The Dalai Lama

A LIFE OF COMPASSION

by Sheila Rivera

Lerner Publications Company • Minneapolis

Photo Acknowledgments

The photographs in this book are reproduced with the permission of: © C. Geral/Retna Ltd., front cover; © JAYANTA SHAW/Reuters/Corbis, p. 4; © Toronto Star/ZUMA Press, pp. 6, 7; © PETER PARKS/AFP/Getty Images, p. 8; The Collection of the Newark Museum, p. 9; © Galen Rowell/CORBIS, p. 10; © Christine Kolisch/CORBIS, p. 11; © CORBIS, p. 12; © Earl & Nazima Kowall/CORBIS, p. 13; © Bettmann/CORBIS, pp. 14, 18, 19, 22; © Hulton-Deutsch Collection/CORBIS, p. 16; AP/Wide World Photos, pp. 17, 20, 24; © DAVID BEBBER/ Reuters/Corbis, p. 25; © STRDEL/AFP/Getty Images, p. 26.

Text copyright © 2007 by Lerner Publishing Group, Inc.

Lerner Publications Company
A division of Lerner Publishing Group, Inc.
241 First Avenue North
Minneapolis, MN 55401 USA

For reading levels and more information, look up this title at www.lernerbooks.com.

Words in **bold type** are explained in a glossary on page 31.

Library of Congress Cataloging-in-Publication Data

Rivera, Sheila, 1970–
    The Dalai Lama : a life of compassion / by Sheila Rivera.
      p. cm. – (Pull ahead books)
    Includes index.
    ISBN-13: 978-0-8225-6386-0 (alk. paper)
    ISBN-10: 0-8225-6386-X (alk. paper)
    1. Bstan-'dzin-rgya-mtsho, Dalai Lama XIV, 1935–Juvenile literature. 2. Dalai Lamas–Biography–Juvenile literature. I. Title. II. Series.
BQ7935.B777R58 2007
294.3'923092–dc22
                                                2006005517

Manufactured in the United States of America
3 – CG – 11/1/13

Table of Contents

Becoming a Leader 5

Danger 15

Leaving Tibet 21

Talk of Peace 23

Love One Another 27

Dalai Lama Timeline 28

More about the Dalai Lama 30

Websites 30

Glossary 31

Index 32

The Dalai Lama

Becoming a Leader

Do you know who the Dalai Lama is? He is the leader of Tibet. He is also a **religious** leader. The Dalai Lama is a **compassionate** person. He cares about people. He worries when people don't get along. He believes in peace.

The Dalai Lama was born in a small town in Tibet. His parents named him Lhamo Dhondup.

Lhamo Dhondup

When Lhamo was a little boy, some **Buddhist monks** came to his house. These religious men knew that Lhamo was special.

Lhamo's parents took him to live with the monks in a **monastery**. This is where monks live and work together.

A monk walks in the monastery where the Dalai Lama lived.

Tibet's government announced that Lhamo was the Dalai Lama. He became the country's religious leader.

The Potala Palace

Two years later, the Dalai Lama went to live at the Potala Palace.

The Dalai Lama spent most of his time studying. He studied religion, art, and many other subjects.

The Dalai Lama learned about this god when he studied religion.

The Dalai Lama liked to talk with the servants at the palace. They told him about the lives of ordinary Tibetans.

A group of Tibetans gather near the palace.

The Dalai Lama could see most of the town from the palace.

The Dalai Lama watched the people in town from his window. He cared about them.

Chinese soldiers moved into Tibet.

Danger

In 1950, China sent **soldiers** to Tibet. They said they would protect the Tibetans from other countries. But the Tibetan people thought that China wanted to rule Tibet.

The Dalai Lama was only 15 years old. But he became the head of Tibet's **government**. He wanted to keep Tibetans safe.

The Dalai Lama sits on his throne.

The Dalai Lama meets with China's leader, Mao Zedong in 1954.

He met with Chinese leaders. He talked about peace between China and Tibet.

Chinese soldiers force Tibetans to leave the palace.

The Chinese said they would help Tibet become a better country. But they did not help.

Chinese leaders said Tibet was part of China. They wanted to rule Tibet.

Soldiers in Tibet carry the Chinese flag.

The Dalai Lama (on the white horse) left Tibet.

Leaving Tibet

People were afraid that the Chinese soldiers would hurt the Dalai Lama. So he decided to move to India with his family. They would be safe in India. But the Dalai Lama still wanted to help his people in Tibet. He did not want them to suffer under Chinese rule.

Chinese soldiers stand guard in Tibet.

Talk of Peace

The Dalai Lama wanted the Chinese soldiers to leave Tibet. He wanted Tibet to be free again. But he did not want his people to fight. The Dalai Lama believed that **violence** was wrong.

The Dalai Lama talked to leaders from other countries. He asked them to help Tibet become free again.

The Dalai Lama asked U.S. president Bill Clinton for help.

A group in Great Britain shows its support for Tibet.

People around the world urged the Chinese to let Tibet rule itself. But the Chinese would not.

The Dalai Lama teaches people to respect one another.

Love One Another

China still controls Tibet. The Dalai Lama hopes that Tibet will be a free country again someday. But he tells Tibetans not to fight. He believes that all people should love and care for one another. He believes in compassion for all people.

DALAI LAMA TIMELINE

1935

Lhamo Dhondup is born on July 6.

1940

He officially becomes Tibet's religious leader.

1937

He goes to live in Kumbum monastery.

1950
China invades
Tibet.

1959
The Dalai Lama
and his family
move to India.

1950
The Dalai Lama
becomes Tibet's ruler
on November 17.

1989
The Dalai Lama wins
the Nobel Peace Prize.

More about the Dalai Lama

● The Dalai Lama won the Nobel Peace Prize in 1989 for his work toward peace.

● The Tibetan people still consider the Dalai Lama their leader even though China controls Tibet.

● The Dalai Lama has lived in India for more than 45 years.

Websites

The Government of Tibet in Exile
http://www.tibet.com/

TibetNet—His Holiness the 14th Dalai Lama of Tibet
http://www.tibet.net/hhdl/eng/

The Website of the Office of His Holiness the 14th Dalai Lama
http://www.dalailama.com/

Glossary

Buddhist monks: men who give up everything to serve the gods of the Buddhist religion

compassionate: sharing someone else's suffering and wanting to help them

government: a group of people who run a country

monastery: a place where monks live and work

religious: believing in and worshipping a god or gods

soldiers: members of an army

violence: using physical force to damage or hurt people or things

Index

childhood, 6–9

China, 15, 17, 19, 27, 28, 30

Clinton, Bill, 24

Great Britian, 25

India, 21, 29, 30

Kumbum monastery, 8, 28

Mao Zedong, 17

monks, 7

Nobel Peace Prize, 29, 30

Potala Palace, 10, 12

Tibet, 5, 6, 9, 14–25, 27–30,